D1109905

Every

SISTER

*should have
a book
like this...*

Other Titles in This Series:

*Every Daughter Should Have a Book like This
to Remind Her How Wonderful She Is*

*Every Mom Should Have a Book like This
Filled with Love and Appreciation*

*Every Son Should Have a Book like This
Filled with Wishes, Love, and
Encouragement*

Copyright © 2008 by Blue Mountain Arts, Inc.

All rights reserved. No part of this publication may be reproduced, stored in a retrieval system or transmitted in any form or by any means, electronic, mechanical, photocopying, recording or otherwise, without the written permission of the publisher.

All writings are by Douglas Pagels except as noted.

Library of Congress Control Number: 2007937320
ISBN: 978-1-59842-197-2

▌ and Blue Mountain Press are registered in U.S. Patent and Trademark Office. Certain trademarks are used under license.

Acknowledgments appear on page 72.

Printed in China.
First Printing: 2008

✪ This book is printed on recycled paper.

This book is printed on fine quality, laid embossed, 80 lb. paper. This paper has been specially produced to be acid free (neutral pH) and contains no groundwood or unbleached pulp. It conforms with the requirements of the American National Standards Institute, Inc., so as to ensure that this book will last and be enjoyed by future generations.

Blue Mountain Arts, Inc.
P.O. Box 4549, Boulder, Colorado 80306

Every
SISTER
should have
a book
like this

to let her know
what a
blessing she is

Douglas Pagels

Blue Mountain Press ™
Boulder, Colorado

Contents

Remember What Goldie Said...

The relationship between siblings is about as deep as you can go.... No one on the planet will ever know you better than your sibling. They know the good parts, the bad parts, and the secrets. It is a very powerful and valuable relationship. Don't let it slip through your fingers. It is like going home in your heart.

— Goldie Hawn

We share an understanding that goes beyond what two friends can share. There are things I can tell you that I can't say to anyone else... and I think that you feel the same way about me. I am comforted by that thought and by the knowledge that — no matter what happens — I'll always have you, and you'll always have me to talk to, to confide in, and to walk with in every tomorrow.

Everyone needs someone who is always there and always caring. Everyone needs someone who is just a touch or a card or a phone call away. Someone with whom you can share everything that's in your heart or simply talk about the day in the way that only the two of you can.

Everyone needs someone to encourage them; to believe in them; to give a pat on the back when things have gone right... and a shoulder to cry on when they haven't. Everyone needs someone to remind them to keep trying and that it will all work out.

In our own special way, I hope we can always be that someone, that shoulder, and that support for each other.

In life's quiet times, when I'm alone with my thoughts, I think of all the appreciation I have for you. It brings me a lot of gratitude to think of how strong and sure our family ties are, and to know that in the course of time, we will keep adding to our story and filling it with more caring and togetherness.

Remember What Fran Said...

"*Okay, will you please call me if you need me?*"
"*I will.*"
"*Any time of the day or night, I'm here for you.*"
"*I know.*"
"*I love you.*"
"*I love you, too.*"

— Fran Drescher
to her sister, Nadine

You know me better than anyone else.

You know my life story, my hopes and dreams, my innermost secrets, and all the things that most people could never know in a million years.

You know what makes me happy. You know what makes me sad. You understand where I'm coming from and how I want my life to go.

I know so many of those same things about you. It sets the stage for a very unique connection. It's a place where we are free to be human beings — who don't always get it right, but who continue to find acceptance, hope, and encouragement.

Our relationship exists in a place where we wish together on one another's stars, no matter where we are.

Remember What Joy Said...

It is amazing how two sisters can be brought up in the same family, but live very different lives.

— Joy Harjo

The Story of Two Very Different Sisters

One is here, one is there. One is a little taller than the other. Two different styles of hair, two different outlooks on life, two very different views from their windows. Both have different tomorrows ahead...

Each is unique in so many ways. Each has her own story, with all the busy things going on in the present. Each has different work to do and different demands on the day. Each has a separate destination and a distinctly different path to get there.

But, for all the things that might be different and unique about them...

these two sisters will always share so much. They will always be the best of family __and__ friends, entwined together, through all the days of their lives. Their love will always be very special: gentle and joyful when it can be, strong and giving when it needs to be, reminding them, no matter how different their stories turn out...

They share the incredibly precious gift of being "sisters." And when you think of some of the best things this world has to offer, a blessing like that is really... what it's all about.

Remember What Michelle Said...

*K*aren and I are different all right, but we know each other through and through. I swear I can always tell what she's thinking... and she seems to know when I'm going to call her. If she goes out, she'll leave a message for me on her answering machine: "If this is you, Michelle..."

Karen has always been my closest buddy and my best supporter. She's been a big part of my success... Without Karen around all the time, it would have taken me a lot longer to know who "myself" really was.

We knew we could always count on each other, and together we were an unbeatable team.

— Michelle Kwan

I Have a Sister
Who Is Also...

A precious part of everything
that family means to me.
An understanding soul I know
I can talk to about anything.

A person I want to stay close to
no matter how far apart we live,
what happens in the days ahead,
or what the years may bring.

A gift for which I am exceedingly
  grateful and someone with whom
  I will share so much till the end
  of time. Every lucky person has a few
  special blessings they receive in their life.

And you, my sister,
  have been one of mine.

Remember What Alicia Said...

No words will ever do
a sister's love justice.
I know you understand
what I'm saying. There's
no one like you.

— Alicia Keys

Beautiful Things
That Are True About You

You're a one-of-a-kind treasure, uniquely here in this space and time. You are here to shine in your own wonderful way, sharing your smile in the best way you can, and remembering all the while that a little light somewhere makes a brighter light everywhere. You can — and you do — make a wonderful contribution to this world...

You have qualities within you that many people would love to have, and those who really and truly know you... are so glad that they do. You have a big heart and a good and sensitive soul. You are gifted with thoughts and ways of seeing things that only special people know.

You are something — and someone — very special. You really are. No one else in this entire world is exactly like you, and there are so many beautiful things about you.

I Am Very Glad
I Have a Sister like You

On more occasions than I can count,
I have relied on my closeness with you
to offset the difficult days in my life.

You are a comfort and an inspiration
to me. Your voice on the phone is the
best medicine anyone ever invented.
Your concern comes from the heart...
and your encouragement and caring
just have to be some of the nicest
things anyone has ever received.

Remember What Al & Debra Said...

*I wanted to tell my sister...
she is my best friend.*

— Al Roker

*I... feel genuinely sorry for
men who have grown up
without at least one sister.*

— Debra Ginsberg

To you:

For keeping my spirits up.
For never letting me down.
For being here for me.
For knowing I'm there for you.

For bringing so many smiles my way.
For being sensitive to my needs.
For knowing just what to say.
For listening better than anyone else.

For bringing me laughter.
For bringing me light.
For understanding so much about me.
For trusting me with so much about you.

For being the best.
For being so beautiful.

I don't know what I'd do
*   ...without you.*

Remember What Donna Said...

I *can't imagine what it would be like not to have a sister to support me, to tell me the truth, to be there for me whatever it was I needed....*

When we were kids, we took it for granted that there was always a sister on the other end of the teeter-totter. Now I realize what that really means.

— *Donna Masiejczyk*

In your happiest and most exciting moments, my heart will celebrate and smile beside you. In your lowest lows, my love will be there to keep you warm, to give you strength, and to remind you that your sunshine is sure to come again.

In your moments of accomplishment, I will be filled so full of pride that I may have a hard time keeping the feeling inside me.

In your moments of disappointment, I will be a shoulder to cry on, a hand to hold, and a love that will gently enfold you until everything's okay. In your gray days, I will help you search, one by one, for the colors of the rainbow.

Sister, Do You Know What You Are?

You are one of the most wonderful people I will ever have the privilege of knowing.

I really mean that. The older I get, the more I understand how rare it is to be blessed with a sister like you. You're unique in so many ways, and there are very few things in life that even come close to bringing me as much happiness as you do.

You never cease to amaze me. There are so many moments when I am quietly in awe of you... of the joy you inspire, of the serenity you share, and of all the great things that just seem to naturally be a part of you. It's so easy and so nice... being with you. It opens my eyes to all the wonderful qualities about you. I see goodness and kindness there. I see compassion and understanding.

And I never fail to see a twinkle in your eyes... a gentle reminder to me that I am in the company of someone who has a big heart and a beautiful ability to make each day a good one...

I know you're probably going to feel a little embarrassed to hear all the praises I am singing about you, but you deserve all these praises... and many, many more. I'll always think the world of you. I'll cherish all the memories and appreciate the closeness and thank my lucky stars for everything.

So, please... don't ever forget:

I think you are one of the most precious people this world will ever be blessed with.

Remember What Barbara Said...

What is a sister?

She is your mirror, shining back at you with a world of possibilities. She is your witness, who sees you at your worst and best, and loves you anyway. She is your partner in crime, your midnight companion, someone who knows when you're smiling, even in the dark. She is your teacher, your defense attorney, your personal press agent, even your shrink. Some days, she's the reason you wish you were an only child. But most of the time her very existence creates a sense of acceptance, of community, of tenderness....

— Barbara Alpert

At Home in My Heart

Even if the times of our lives should find us many miles apart, you will never be alone. I will always be there with you, in some special way that only siblings can be. And you will always be quietly, reassuringly, here with me.

The things you want to come true for you... those things will be my hopes, too. Your history will be my history. And many of your memories will parallel those of my own.

And any time we choose to go there, my closeness with you and your closeness with me will meet on a bridge that will happily take us all the way back home.

Remember What Elizabeth Said...

We are each other's reference point at our turning points. And the dance between us is also a delicate balance of influence, between leader and led, teacher and taught, soother and soothed. We alternately give a shoulder and need one.

— Elizabeth Fishel

In the dance of life, sisters are the people who encourage you to be your best, who like you for who you are, who remind you what steps to take when you've forgotten the way, and who help you rest assured that your secrets are safe and your hopes are in good hands.

They help to balance things out, they keep you on your toes, they make you smile even when you're stumbling through life, and the stories, support, and laughter they bring to the years feel more like music to your ears than just about anything.

When Issues Come Up and Problems Arise

When family members have differences, they're doing something that's perfectly acceptable to do.

They're being human.

Sisters and siblings, parents and children, everyone in the family dynamic has the possibility for something to go wrong at some point.

We live in a difficult, unpredictable world. Life can be so hard sometimes. We've all got roles and responsibilities. We're all juggling so many things.

We're all trying to deal with pressures and stresses that change on a daily basis. Sometimes those things affect our most important relationships.

But the sweet, simple, absolute truth is that the differences between people don't have to last. Especially between siblings...

Life is too short for problems to divide two people who will be family companions all their lives long.

Love is the candle you light to chase away the darkness of a misunderstanding.

May the two of us always let that light shine in our hearts and warm our lives.

Remember What Claudia Said...

We always thought that being [sisters] was the greatest blessing on this earth. There is nothing I could do, no disagreement I could have that would make my sisters not love me. We belong to each other and that is inviolate. We each contribute to the solidity of our bond by being there when we're needed. By carrying our own weight. You don't mess with that kind of stuff. You invest in it.

— Claudia Pharis

"Gratitude" is one of the nicest feelings a heart can have. It's a feeling that comes along for a very special reason — and it's a lovely thought that never goes away once it enters in. It joins together with precious memories and grateful hopes. Gratitude lives on, not for just a moment or a day, but through all the seasons that lie ahead.

This Is to Thank You...

For all those times when I never could have managed without a sister like you.

For being such a constant in my life — amidst all the changes the rest of my world goes through.

For being remarkable in your qualities, inspiring in your thoughts, and caring in your heart.

For being the one I will always feel close to, whether we're together or miles apart.

For being my definition of "special," and for proving it over and over again.

Remember What Kelly Said...

My sisters are guaranteed friends for life. I know it doesn't necessarily have to be that way. But that's how it is with us. We have friends with sisters who don't get along. Like them, we know what buttons to push. But out of respect we don't push them. There's never a reason to hurt your sisters. Never was, never will be.

— Kelly Turlington

If you could see yourself reflected in my eyes, you would see someone who makes my heart just smile inside. You would catch a glimpse of a sister who has been such a wonderful influence on my life and who keeps on making a beautiful difference in my days...

If you could hear the words I would love to share, you would be able to listen to a special tribute to you, one that sings your praises and speaks of an unending gratitude and describes how much I'll always appreciate you.

If you could imagine one of the nicest gifts anyone could ever receive, you would begin to understand what your presence in my life has meant to me.

A sister can make your whole day just by saying something that no one else could have said. Sometimes you feel like the two of you share a secret language that others can't tune in to.

When your feelings come from deep inside and need to be spoken to someone you know you can trust, you share them with your sister.

When good news comes, she is the first one you turn to. When feelings overflow and tears need to fall, a sister helps you through it all.

Remember What
Robert Said...

Sisters at one and the same time can be girlfriends, listening ears, best friends, shopping collaborators, just plain buddies, confidants, rivals, and much, much more....

Sisters, whatever you may say or think, function as one of the best support-systems/safety-nets in a world churned by the chaos of change all around us. Just the fact that a sister will be there is a great comfort.

— Robert Strand

In This Crazy World We Live in, It's Nice to Know That Some Things Will Never Change...

No matter what is happening in the world.
No matter what worries or frustrations creep in.
No matter what glad or sad tidings come your way.
No matter how many bills come in the mail.
No matter how good or bad the news of the day.
No matter whether the weather is beautiful or not.
No matter how many times your smile gets lost.
No matter how difficult or demanding things can be.
No matter what is happening anywhere at any time...

You will always be in my heart. You will always be in my thoughts. And I'll always be wishing I could find a way to remind you... that your happiness is very important to me.

I know that life can be hard sometimes, and that the world can be a crazy place. But I want you to remember that the two of us will always do what we can to make things better... and my love will walk beside you, from now until forever.

Remember What This Says...

It's as if we are cut from the same fabric. Even though we appear to be sewn in a different pattern, we have a common thread that won't be broken by people or years or distance.

— Anonymous

Sisters share a relationship that is unique and rare and wonderful.

The yesterdays of their lives are threaded together like a friendship quilt, reflecting on scenes they each know so well and which today live on in some of their most beautiful memories.

Their relationship is interwoven with a love that never leaves, with listening and laughing, with comfort and trust, and with more honest communication than almost any two people can share.

You will always have a starring role
in the story of my life.

*You provide laughter and smiles when
my life is like a comedy. (Which, as you
know, is most of the time!)*

*You're there with understanding and
support when it seems like I'm appearing
in a soap opera.*

You help me keep things in perspective when I feel like I'm in the middle of a reality show.

You're happy for me when life is like a romance.

And your wonderful, kind, caring spirit always manages to be there for me when things seem like they're going to turn into a tragedy...

I have so many what-would-I-ever-do-
without-you moments in my life.

And I'd just like to thank you, with all
my heart, for being the incredibly
important star that you are... to me.

Remember What Vikki Said...

Whether your sister's role in your life has been to clear the path, follow in your footsteps, walk by your side, or any of the myriad other possibilities, you were fashioned by the type of sister relationship you experienced.

— *Vikki Stark*

A Sister like You
Is Such a Wonderful Gift

There have been at least a thousand times when I have thanked my lucky stars for you.

You are such a wonderful example of how to live a life that brightens the days of everyone around you.

You are a steady stream of support, a reassuring feeling that is always with me, and a gift whose value is immeasurable.

You are beautiful in more ways than you know, and you always will be.

You have been my sister since the beginning, you will be my friend forever, and you are someone I treasure more than my words can even begin to express.

Remember What Nicole Said...

I'll do anything for her. Anything. It makes me cry I love her so much. You know, I think when you have that kind of love in your family, it keeps you very available and trusting of others.

— *Nicole Kidman*

A Message to My Sister: I'm Going to Be Here for You, No Matter What

When you need someone to turn to, I'll be here for you. I will do whatever it takes and give as much as I can... to help you find your smile and get you back on steady ground again.

When you just need to talk, I will listen with my heart. And I will do my best to hear the things you may want to say, but can't quite find the words for...

I will never betray the trust you put in me. All I will do is keep on caring and doing my best to see you through. If there are decisions to be made, I may offer a direction to go in. If there are tears to be dried, I will tenderly dry them.

I want you to feel completely at ease about reaching out to me. And don't ever forget this: you couldn't impose on me if you tried. It simply isn't possible.

Your happiness and peace of mind are so closely interwoven with mine that they are inseparable. I will truly, deeply, and completely care about you every day...

You can count on that. I hope it will invite a little more serenity into your life to know you're not alone, and I hope it will encourage a brighter day to shine through.

I'm not going anywhere. I promise.

Unless it's to come to your side and to hold out a hand... to you.

Remember What Marcia Said...

She understands you intuitively because she had the same parents and shared your childhood. She laughed and cried with you through all your early adventures: family outings and holidays, summers at the beach, shopping expeditions, getting through school....

She gives you what no one else in the world can give you — a lasting connection to your childhood and family. Your sister shares your memories of all the important people and events.... She's the one person you have for your entire life.

— Marcia Millman

I would give anything for these wishes
to keep coming true for us
all our lives...

That we may always be more than close.
That nothing will ever come between
the bond of love we're blessed with.
That we will celebrate our similarities,
honor the things that make each of
us unique, and quietly realize that
every part of the circle of our lives
is a special, precious gift.

That I will always be here for you,
as you will be for me.
That we will listen with love...

That we will share everything that
    wants to — and needs to — be shared.
That we will care unconditionally.

That we will trust so much, and we will
    talk things out.
That we will nurture each other's
    spirit and warm each other's soul.
That even when no one else knows
    what's going on inside...
    you and I will gently understand.

...And that wherever you go, you will be
    in my heart, and my hand
    will be in your hand.

And Remember
What I Said...

Within my heart,
in a certain place where
my favorite memories
and my happiest hopes
and my nicest thoughts are...

there is a space that belongs
just to you.

— Douglas Pagels

As this book comes to a close, I just want to say a special thanks to you. It's one that hasn't been spoken nearly enough through the years, but it has been right here in my heart... and it always will be.

For all the days behind us, and for all the days to come, I want you to know... how blessed I am and how lucky I've been...

to have a sister like you.

ACKNOWLEDGMENTS

We gratefully acknowledge the permission granted by the following authors, publishers, and authors' representatives to reprint poems or excerpts from their publications.

G.P. Putnam's Sons, a division of Penguin Group (USA), Inc., for "The relationship between siblings..." from A LOTUS GROWS IN THE MUD by Goldie Hawn. Copyright © 2005 by Illume, LLC. And for "No words will ever do..." from TEARS FOR WATER: SONGBOOK OF POEMS AND LYRICS by Alicia Keys. Copyright © 2004 by Lellow Brands, Inc. All rights reserved.

Warner Books, Inc., for "'Okay, will you please call me...'" from CANCER SCHMANCER by Fran Drescher. Copyright © 2002 by Fran Drescher. Reprinted by permission of Warner Books, Inc. All rights reserved.

Joy Harjo for "It is amazing how two sisters..." from SISTER TO SISTER, edited by Patricia Foster. Copyright © 1995 by Joy Harjo. All rights reserved.

Scholastic, Inc., for "Karen and I are different all right..." from HEART OF A CHAMPION: MY STORY by Michelle Kwan. Copyright © 1997 by Michelle Kwan Corp. All rights reserved.

Scribner, an imprint of Simon & Schuster Adult Publishing Group, for "I wanted to tell my sister..." from DON'T MAKE ME STOP THIS CAR! by Al Roker. Copyright © 2000 by Al Roker. All rights reserved.

HarperCollins Publishers for "I... feel genuinely sorry for..." from ABOUT MY SISTERS by Debra Ginsberg. Copyright © 2004 by Debra Ginsberg. All rights reserved.

Running Press, a member of Perseus Book Group, for "I can't imagine what it would..." by Donna Masiejczyk, "We always thought that being..." by Claudia Pharis, and "My sisters are guaranteed friends..." by Kelly Turlington from SISTERS: 10th ANNIVERSARY EDITION by Carol Saline. Copyright © 1994 by Carol Saline. All rights reserved.

Berkley Publishing Group, a division of Penguin Group (USA), Inc., for "What is a sister?" from NO FRIEND LIKE A SISTER by Barbara Alpert. Copyright © 1996 by Barbara Alpert. All rights reserved.

Conari Press, an imprint of Red Wheel/Weiser, Newburyport, MA and San Francisco, CA, for "We are each other's reference point..." from SISTERS by Elizabeth Fishel. Copyright © 1997 by Elizabeth Fishel. All rights reserved.

New Leaf Press for "Sisters at one and the same time..." from MOMENTS FOR SISTERS by Robert Strand. Copyright © 1995 by New Leaf Press. All rights reserved.

The McGraw-Hill Companies for "Whether your sister's role..." from MY SISTER, MY SELF by Vikki Stark. Copyright © 2007 by Vikki Stark. All rights reserved.

Jeanne Marie Laskas for "I'll do anything for her..." by Nicole Kidman from "A Mission of Love." Originally published in *Ladies' Home Journal*. Copyright © 2006 by Jeanne Marie Laskas. All rights reserved.

Harvest Books, an imprint of Harcourt, Inc., for "She understands you intuitively..." from THE PERFECT SISTER by Marcia Millman. Copyright © 2004 by Marcia Millman. All rights reserved.

A careful effort has been made to trace the ownership of selections used in this anthology in order to obtain permission to reprint copyrighted material and give proper credit to the copyright owners. If any error or omission has occurred, it is completely inadvertent, and we would like to make corrections in future editions provided that written notification is made to the publisher:

BLUE MOUNTAIN ARTS, INC., P.O. Box 4549, Boulder, Colorado 80306.